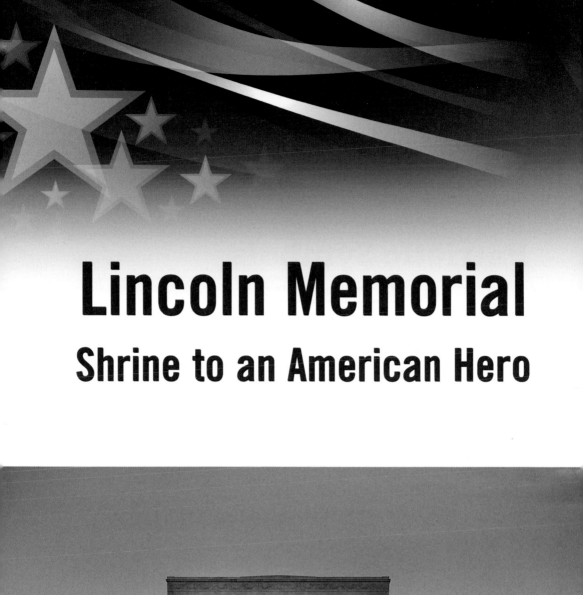

Lincoln Memorial

Shrine to an American Hero

Patriotic Symbols
of America

The Alamo: Symbol of Freedom
American Flag: The Story of Old Glory
Bald Eagle: The Story of Our National Bird
Confederate Flag: Controversial Symbol of the South
The Declaration of Independence: Forming a New Nation
Ellis Island: The Story of a Gateway to America
Independence Hall: Birthplace of Freedom
Jefferson Memorial: A Monument to Greatness
Liberty Bell: Let Freedom Ring
Lincoln Memorial: Shrine to an American Hero
Mount Rushmore: Memorial to Our Greatest Presidents
The Pledge of Allegiance: Story of One Indivisible Nation
Rock 'n' Roll: Voice of American Youth
The Star-Spangled Banner: Story of Our National Anthem
Statue of Liberty: A Beacon of Welcome and Hope
Uncle Sam: International Symbol of America
The U.S. Constitution: Government by the People
Vietnam Veterans Memorial: Remembering a Generation and a War
Washington Monument: Memorial to a Founding Father
The White House: The Home of the U.S. President

Lincoln Memorial
Shrine to an American Hero

Hal Marcovitz

Mason Crest
Philadelphia

Mason Crest
450 Parkway Drive, Suite D
Broomall, PA 19008
www.masoncrest.com

Printed and bound in the United States of America.

CPSIA Compliance Information: Batch #PSA2014. For further information, contact Mason Crest at 1-866-MCP-Book.

Publisher's note: all quotations in this book come from original sources, and contain the spelling and grammatical inconsistencies of the original text.

First printing
1 3 5 7 9 8 6 4 2

Library of Congress Cataloging-in-Publication Data

on file at the Library of Congress

ISBN: 978-1-4222-3127-2 (hc)
ISBN: 978-1-4222-8750-7 (ebook)

Patriotic Symbols of America series ISBN: 978-1-4222-3117-3

Contents

Patriotic Symbols and American History   **6**
Introduction by Barry Moreno

1. Marian Anderson   **9**

2. A Monument For Lincoln   **13**

3. A Matchless Tribute   **21**

4. Enshrined Forever   **29**

5. Free at Last   **35**

Chronology   **42**

Series Glossary   **43**

Further Reading   **45**

Internet Resources   **45**

Index   **46**

KEY ICONS TO LOOK FOR:

Text-dependent questions: These questions send the reader back to the text for more careful attention to the evidence presented there.

Words to understand: These words with their easy-to-understand definitions will increase the reader's understanding of the text, while building vocabulary skills.

Series glossary of key terms: This back-of-the book glossary contains terminology used throughout this series. Words found here increase the reader's ability to read and comprehend higher-level books and articles in this field.

Research projects: Readers are pointed toward areas of further inquiry connected to each chapter. Suggestions are provided for projects that encourage deeper research and analysis.

Sidebars: This boxed material within the main text allows readers to build knowledge, gain insights, explore possibilities, and broaden their perspectives by weaving together additional information to provide realistic and holistic perspectives.

Patriotic Symbols and American History

Symbols are not merely ornaments to admire—they also tell us stories. If you look at one of them closely, you may want to find out why it was made and what it truly means. If you ask people who live in the society in which the symbol exists, you will learn some things. But by studying the people who created that symbol and the reasons why they made it, you will understand the deepest meanings of that symbol.

The United States owes its identity to great events in history, and the most remarkable of our patriotic symbols are rooted in these events. The struggle for independence from Great Britain gave America the Declaration of Independence, the Liberty Bell, the American flag, and other images of freedom. The War of 1812 gave the young country a song dedicated to the flag, "The Star-Spangled Banner," which became our national anthem. Nature gave the country its national animal, the bald eagle. These symbols established the identity of the new nation, and set it apart from the nations of the Old World.

To be emotionally moving, a symbol must strike people with a sense of power and unity. But it often takes a long time for a new symbol to be accepted by all the people, especially if there are older symbols that have gradually lost popularity. For example, the image of Uncle Sam has replaced Brother Jonathan, an earlier representation of the national will, while the Statue of Liberty has replaced Columbia, a woman who represented liberty to Americans in the early 19th century. Since then, Uncle Sam and the Statue of Liberty have endured and have become cherished icons of America.

Of all the symbols, the Statue of Liberty has perhaps the most curious story, for unlike other symbols, Americans did not create her. She was created by the French, who then gave her to America. Hence, she represented not what Americans thought of their country but rather what the French thought of America. It was many years before Americans decided to accept this French goddess of Liberty as a symbol for the United States and its special role among the nations: to spread freedom and enlighten the world.

This series of books is valuable because it presents the story of each of America's great symbols in a freshly written way and will contribute to the students' knowledge and awareness of them. It it to be hoped that this information will awaken an abiding interest in American history, as well as in the meanings of American symbols.

—Barry Moreno,
librarian and historian
Ellis Island/Statue of Liberty National Monument

 Words to Understand

capital—the city that serves as the official center of a government for a state or nation.

contralto—the lowest female voice; tone is found between soprano and tenor.

First Lady—the wife of a president of the United States or a governor of a state.

Marian Anderson, a popular opera singer of the early 20th century, performs at the Lincoln Memorial on Easter Sunday 1939. Although President Abraham Lincoln had freed the slaves nearly 75 years earlier, Anderson and other African Americans continued to suffer from racial discrimination well into the 20th century.

Marian Anderson

The plight of black Americans seemed hopeless at the close of the 19th century. The Civil War had meant freedom from slavery for southern blacks, but in the years following the war many southern states had passed "Jim Crow laws" that prevented blacks from voting and sharing in other rights guaranteed to white Americans. Blacks in the North faced discrimination as well. Few African Americans were able to win good jobs or pursue quality educations.

Nevertheless, some blacks were able to excel, giving hope to others that, in America, they too would have a chance to escape poverty. For many black citizens, Marian Anderson would serve as an example that in America, a person's talent meant far more than the color of a person's skin.

Marian Anderson was born into a typical black home in the 1890s. When she was six years old, Anderson started singing in the choir of the Union Baptist Church in Philadelphia. It didn't take long for audiences to recognize her incredible *contralto* voice. By the time she was 16, Anderson was singing on stages in New York City. She soon accepted invitations to perform in Europe. There, the promoters of concerts and operas were anxious to display her talents. In America, however, few promoters were willing to let her onto their stages.

In 1939, theatrical producer Sol Hurok heard Anderson perform in Paris and decided that her beautiful voice would appeal to Americans, regardless of her race. He booked Anderson on a nationwide tour of America's great concert halls.

In Washington, D. C., the nation's *capital*, Anderson was booked to perform in the 2,000-seat auditorium of Constitution Hall. This is the headquarters of the Daughters of the American Revolution (DAR), an organization of women whose ancestors had fought in America's War for Independence.

But as the date of the concert grew near, Hurok was told by the DAR that Anderson would not be allowed to perform in Constitution Hall—that no "coloreds" were permitted on the stage. "I was saddened and ashamed," Anderson recalled later. "I felt that the behavior of the DAR stemmed from a lack of understanding. They were doing something that was neither sensible nor good."

Word of the DAR's decision to bar Anderson from Constitution Hall spread quickly through Washington. When Eleanor Roosevelt, the *First Lady*, learned of the DAR's action, she was outraged. She was a member of the DAR herself, but decided that she could no longer belong to an organization that would show a bias against race. And so Mrs. Roosevelt resigned from the group. She urged Interior Secretary Harold L. Ickes to permit Anderson to give a concert on the steps of the Lincoln Memorial.

On April 9, 1939–Easter Sunday—75,000 people gathered on the National Mall in Washington to attend a free concert performed by Marian Anderson. The singer stepped onto the stage that had been erected on the Lincoln Memorial's steps, taking her place behind a battery of microphones that would broadcast the concert to a national radio audience of millions.

She closed her eyes and sang the words, "My country 'tis of thee, sweet land of liberty."

Marian Anderson had chosen to sing "America."

 Text-Dependent Question
What were "Jim Crow" laws?

Research Project
Why would Eleanor Roosevelt, a white woman, care that Marian Anderson was not permitted to sing at the DAR's Constitution Hall? Do some research to find out what causes Mrs. Roosevelt was involved in, and how she supported those causes throughout her life.

Words to Understand

architect—a person who designs buildings.

assassin—A person who kills a prominent person, often for political reasons.

Capitol—a building in Washington, D.C., where Congress passes laws and conducts other business. Some states house their legislatures in buildings called Capitols, also.

Congress—the lawmaking branch of the American government.

emancipate—to free a slave from bondage.

obelisk—a shaft of stone that tapers at the peak.

sculptor—a person who fashions statues or other three-dimensional works of art.

After Abraham Lincoln was elected president in 1860, many of the Southern states decided to leave the Union. From 1861 to 1865, Lincoln tried to bring an end to the Civil War without dissolving the Union. He was ultimately successful, and his commitment to restore and secure a permanent union and to end slavery changed the United States forever.

A Monument for Lincoln

On April 14, 1865, as the Civil War was entering its final days, *assassin* John Wilkes Booth made his way into Ford's Theater in Washington and shot President Abraham Lincoln.

A somber period swept over the nation as millions of people mourned the president who *emancipated* the slaves and kept the Union together during four years of Civil War. *Congress* soon made plans to honor the slain president. In March 1867, the nation's lawmakers established the Lincoln Monument Association with the aim to build a national memorial to the 16th president.

The association turned first to Clarke Mills, the most prominent American *sculptor* of the era. Mills designed a 70-foot monument that would include an enormous sculpture of Lincoln surrounded by 31 Union Army foot soldiers and six mounted cavalrymen. The Lincoln Monument Association quickly accepted Mills' design, but Congress balked at providing money for the project. Instead, Congress authorized the nation's postmasters to collect voluntary donations from people for the purpose of financing construction of the monument.

The postmasters collected little money. Part of the problem was that the monument to Abraham Lincoln was in competition for private money with the Washington Monument. Construction of the *obelisk* honoring the nation's first president had started in 1848 but had stalled during the Civil War. Now that the war was over, sponsors of the partially finished monument on the National Mall were again seeking donations but were making little progress. Eventually, the United States Army Corps of Engineers would take on the job of completing the Washington Monument, which was finally finished in 1885.

The Lincoln Monument Association received no such help from the federal government. Soon, the idea of building a memorial to the Great Emancipator was forgotten. The Lincoln Monument Association disbanded, and the plans of Clarke Mills were forgotten.

Years passed before the idea was revived. In 1911, U.S. Senator Shelby Cullom of Illinois, who had known and admired Lincoln, drafted a Senate bill authorizing the use of federal money for the construction of a Lincoln

Memorial. Cullom wrote: "Abraham Lincoln, greatest of Americans, greatest of men, emancipator, martyr. His service to his country has not been equaled by any American citizen, not even by Washington. His name and life has been an inspiration to me from my earliest recollection."

Cullom found an important ally in the House of Representatives in Speaker Joseph G. Cannon, who persuaded his fellow House members to support Cullom's plan. The United States Congress is composed of two chambers—the House and the Senate—and all legislation must be approved by both chambers as well as the president in order to become law.

VITAL FIGURE: Shelby M. Cullom

Born on November 22, 1829, Shelby M. Cullom shared a common hometown with Abraham Lincoln: Springfield, Illinois. Like Lincoln, Cullom practiced law in Springfield and later went on to represent Springfield in the U.S. House of Representatives. In 1876, he was elected to the first of two terms as governor of Illinois.

In 1883, Cullom returned to Washington as a senator, where he served until his death on January 28, 1914—just two weeks before the groundbreaking ceremony for the Lincoln Memorial, the project he had guided through the Senate.

By the time of his death, Cullom was one of the few political leaders remaining in Washington who could say they knew Lincoln personally.

"I knew him intimately in Springfield," Cullom wrote. "I heard him utter his simple farewell to his friends and neighbors when he departed to assume a task greater than any president had been called upon to assume in our history."

Once the House and Senate agreed to the legislation authorizing the Lincoln Memorial, it was sent to President William Howard Taft for his approval. Taft signed the bill on February 19, 1911.

The bill drafted by Cullom and Cannon set aside $2 million for the memorial. This was the most Congress had ever spent on a public monument. The Washington Monument, completed just 26 years before, had cost the taxpayers just a little more than $1 million.

Make Connections

The Cannon House Office Building in Washington, where many members of Congress maintain their offices, was named in honor of Congressman Joseph Cannon.

The bill signed by Taft established a "Lincoln Memorial Commission" to oversee construction of the memorial, and designated the president of the United States to head the commission. President Taft held the first meeting of the commission on March 4, 1911. Also joining the commission that day were Cullom, Cannon, and four other members of Congress.

The first order of business for the commission would be to pick the design. For the next two years, the commission was flooded with ideas—some quite grand, some clearly too large and expensive to be given serious consideration. The commission members agreed that the final design should in some way incorporate a statue in the image of the slain president.

The commission also needed to find a site for the

monument's construction. They looked at several sites in Washington, and soon found themselves drawn to a tract of land at the western end of the National Mall.

Back in the 1790s, French engineer Pierre Charles L'Enfant had worked closely with George Washington to plan the new federal city. They set aside land for a 146-acre park. The area was to contain shrines, the president's residence—eventually to be known as the White House—and the U.S. *Capitol*. The park soon became known as the National Mall.

The Capitol sits at the eastern end of the National Mall. The White House was erected at the northern end of the Mall. The Washington Monument is in the center of the Mall. At the time, there were no buildings at the western or southern tips of the Mall. (In 1939, a memorial to Thomas Jefferson would be erected at the southern end of the Mall.)

Many people felt the area, which ended at the Potomac River, would be an ideal site. John Hay, a former secretary of state who had once served on Lincoln's staff, wrote to the commission members in favor of Potomac Park. His letter said, "His monument should stand alone, remote from the common habitations of man, apart from the

Make Connections

In addition to the Lincoln Memorial, the National Mall includes monuments to Presidents Franklin Delano Roosevelt, Thomas Jefferson, and George Washington, and memorials to the Americans who served in World War II, the Korean Conflict, and the Vietnam War.

business and turmoil of the city, isolated, distinguished and serene."

Locating the memorial on the banks of the Potomac meant that the structure would overlook Arlington National Cemetery, across the river in Virginia. Many of the soldiers who died in the Civil War were buried in Arlington.

What's more, by placing the Lincoln Memorial at the far end of the Mall, the commission found it could create a truly unique shrine to America's two greatest leaders. Within the Mall, visitors would find the 555-foot obelisk built as a monument to George Washington, the father of his country, as well as a solemn memorial to Abraham Lincoln, the Great Emancipator. On February 3, 1912, the Lincoln Memorial Commission officially designated Potomac Park as the site for the Lincoln Memorial.

Although the commission now had a site, it still did not have a design. So commission members turned to *architect* Henry Bacon. He was hired by the Lincoln Memorial Commission on February 1, 1913.

Bacon designed the memorial to resemble the Parthenon in Greece—it would be a great, open building surrounded by wide steps. Encircling the memorial would be 36 columns—one for each state at the time of Lincoln's death. Names of the states would be carved above the columns.

Inside the memorial, a visitor would find a huge interior space split into three chambers. Etched into the

Architect Henry Bacon based the design of the Lincoln Memorial on the Parthenon in Athens, Greece. As a young man, Bacon had visited Athens while studying architecture in Europe.

walls of the side chambers would be the words from Lincoln's two greatest speeches—the Gettysburg Address and the Second Inaugural Address. Also, two large colorful murals would decorate the interior walls of the chambers.

Finally, in the center chamber of the memorial, Bacon envisioned a grand statue carved in the image of Abraham Lincoln.

Text-Dependent Question
What structures were located on the National Mall at the time a site was chosen for the Lincoln Memorial?

Research Project
The land where Arlington National Cemetery is located was once owned by a famous American who served in the Civil War. Find out who owned the Arlington plantation, and why the property was used as a cemetery for Union soldiers killed during the Civil War.

IN THIS TEMPLE
AS IN THE HEARTS OF THE PEOPLE
FOR WHOM HE SAVED THE UNION
THE MEMORY OF ABRAHAM LINCOLN
IS ENSHRINED FOREVER

Words to Understand

mural—an artwork applied to a wall or ceiling.

This large statue of Abraham Lincoln looks out from the center of the monument. Over its head is carved, "In this temple, as in the hearts of the people for whom he saved the Union, the memory of Abraham Lincoln is enshrined forever."

A Matchless Tribute

Not everyone wanted to model the Lincoln Memorial on the Greek Parthenon. After all, Lincoln was a humble man who was born in a log cabin and learned to read and write by the light of a fire. Critics said the design was too elegant to represent a man from such a simple background.

But one enthusiastic supporter of the memorial was a sculptor named Daniel Chester French. He wrote, "Many people say they are unable to associate Lincoln with a Greek temple, as they believe the memorial to be, but to me nothing else would have been suitable, for the Greeks alone were able to express in their buildings, monuments and statues the highest attributes and the greatest beauty known to man. The memorial tells you just what manner of man you are come to pay homage to; his simplicity, his grandeur and his power."

Work commenced on February 12, 1914, the 105th anniversary of Lincoln's birth. It was a cold, blustery day on the banks of the Potomac River. Nevertheless, a small group of officials bravely stood on the chilly grounds of the National Mall to witness the groundbreaking. One who was absent was Senator Shelby Cullom. He had died two weeks before.

Although the construction was now underway, a sculptor for the statue that would dominate the interior of the monument had yet to be selected. Bacon regarded the statue as the centerpiece of the memorial. He wrote: "The most important object is the statue of Lincoln, which is placed in the center of the Memorial, and by virtue of its imposing position in the place of honor, the gentleness, power and intelligence of the man, expressed as far as possible by the sculptor's art, predominates."

Bacon turned to French, with whom he had worked on a memorial to Lincoln in Nebraska. By the time construction started on the Lincoln Memorial, French was one of America's best-known sculptors. He was called to Washington by Bacon, and together the two men discussed plans for the statue.

After inspecting the plans as well as the work already underway, French decided that Lincoln's image would have to be cast in a sitting position. If he made a statue of Lincoln standing, it would be so tall that visitors to the

VITAL FIGURE: Daniel C. French, sculptor

Daniel Chester French grew up on a Massachusetts farm, learning sculpture by making clay figures of the farm animals. In the 1870s, French moved to New York, where he was trained by several eminent sculptors.

In 1873, French returned to Massachusetts to accept a job to make a bronze sculpture of a minuteman in Concord, Massachusetts. This would commemorate the contribution the minutemen had made to the American Revolution. French's sculpture won him instant and widespread acclaim. For the rest of his career his skills in fashioning public art would be in demand. He would go on to fashion statues for the World's Columbian Exposition in Chicago in 1893, the Boston Public Library in 1904, and the U.S. Customs House in New York in 1907.

French's work came to the attention of Henry Bacon at the Columbian Exposition. Later, the two men worked together on a statue of Abraham Lincoln in Nebraska before collaborating on the Lincoln Memorial in Washington. He died in 1931 at the age of 82.

monument would not be able to see its head. At the end of their meeting, French was offered the contract to carve the statue of Lincoln. He accepted and hurried back to his studio in Massachusetts to begin work.

French began by studying photographs of Lincoln. He also read a great deal about Lincoln. French decided that the great man's most important qualities were his internal strength and compassionate nature. During his research into the life of Lincoln, French found a letter the president had written to the mother of five boys killed in the Civil War. That letter made a deep impression on

French. It read:

> I have been shown in the files of the War Department a statement of the Adjutant-General of Massachusetts that you are the mother of five sons who have died gloriously on the field of battle. I feel how weak and fruitless this must be any words of mine which should attempt to beguile you from the grief of a loss so overwhelming. But I cannot refrain from tendering to you the consolation that may be found in the thanks of the Republic they died to save. I pray that our heavenly father may assuage the anguish of your bereavement, and leave you only the cherished memory of the loved and lost, and the solemn pride that must be yours to have laid so costly a sacrifice upon the altar of freedom.

In October 1916, after completing several small models of the statue, French produced a seven-foot version that showed Bacon as well as members of the Lincoln Memorial Commission exactly what they could expect to be sitting at the center of the monument.

He fashioned Lincoln in a "curule" chair—a formal chair favored by rulers in ancient Rome. French decided such a chair would be more dignified than the folksy easy chairs or rocking chairs Lincoln was known to favor while living in the White House.

Lincoln's left hand was clenched, representing his strength and determination to see the Civil War to its end. His right hand was open to show Lincoln also had a calm and compassionate nature. His face carried a stern expression, to show his ruggedness, but there was also a look of thoughtful concern in his features.

Daniel Chester French works in his studio in Stockbridge, Massachusetts. Behind him is the model he used to create the statue of Lincoln for the Lincoln Memorial.

When Bacon saw the model in French's studio, he immediately approved it. Next, the two men headed to Washington, where they inspected the construction site to get an idea of how big to make the statue. French's original contract for the work specified that the statue be at least 10 feet tall, but the two men quickly agreed that a 10-foot statue would appear tiny inside the massive interior chamber of the memorial. They finally decided that the finished statue should rise 19 feet from the bottom of Lincoln's foot to the top of his head, and that the chair would rest on a pedestal 11 feet high.

To carve the statue, French enlisted the aid of the Piccirillis of New York, brothers whose stone-cutting skills were well known to American sculptors. French had decided the statue would be carved out of marble, but it was so large that there was no way he could find a single block massive enough to accommodate the entire sculpture. So the Piccirillis worked on 28 separate blocks of marble that would eventually be assembled into the final statue at the memorial in Washington.

French and the Piccirillis started work on the statue in November 1918 and completed it a year later. Soon, the pieces were being put together at the memorial. In May 1920, French wrote that the statue of Abraham Lincoln "is now as technically perfect as I can make it."

Meanwhile, Bacon called on the talents of artist Jules V. Guerin to paint two *murals* on the walls of the memorial. The murals would hang high on the north and south walls; each painting was to be 60 feet long by 12 feet high. Each canvas used for the enormous murals weighed 600 pounds.

Above the Gettysburg Address, which was carved into the south wall, Guerin prepared the mural he titled "Emancipation." The mural shows the Angel of Truth flanked on either side by freed slaves. On the north wall, Guerin would hang the mural titled "Reunion," showing the Angel of Truth again, this time joined by representatives of the northern and southern states.

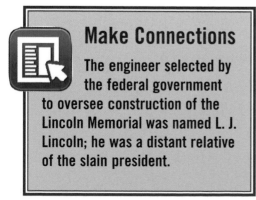

Make Connections

The engineer selected by the federal government to oversee construction of the Lincoln Memorial was named L. J. Lincoln; he was a distant relative of the slain president.

VITAL FIGURE: Jules Guerin, artist

Jules V. Guerin painted "Reunion" and "Emancipation," the two huge murals that decorate the walls of the Lincoln Memorial.

Guerin was born in St. Louis, Missouri, in 1866. He studied art in Paris, and over the years made his home in New Orleans, Louisiana; New York City; and Cairo, Egypt.

In addition to producing the murals for the Lincoln Memorial, Guerin painted murals that decorated the walls of the Pennsylvania Railroad Station in New York, the Federal Reserve Bank in San Francisco, and the Louisiana State Capitol in Baton Rouge. Guerin died in 1946 in Neptune, New Jersey.

Clearly, the murals showed the two great accomplishments of Lincoln's life—the emancipation of the slaves and preservation of the Union.

The Lincoln Memorial was dedicated on May 30, 1922 —Memorial Day. More than 50,000 people crowded onto the National Mall to witness President Warren G. Harding and other officials dedicate the monument to Abraham Lincoln. "This memorial, matchless tribute that it is, is less for Abraham Lincoln than for those of us today, and for those who follow after," Harding said.

Text-Dependent Question
What was the name of the sculptor that created the statue of Abraham Lincoln for the Lincoln Memorial? Where was his studio?

Research Project
The statue of Abraham Lincoln is made from 28 blocks of white Georgia marble. Using the internet, find out how sculptors piece together multiple pieces of stone to create large monuments such as this one. (Videos showing various techniques are available on YouTube.)

 Words to Understand

asbestos—a fibrous mineral used for insulation; has been proven to cause cancer upon repeated inhalation.

foundation—a stone and mortar base built below ground that supports a building, bridge, monument, or other structure.

stalactite—an icicle-shaped deposit, usually hanging from the ceiling of a cave, formed by the dripping of water over stone.

stalagmite—a mound formed on the floor of a cave or underground area, caused by the dripping of water over stone.

Enshrined Forever

The Lincoln Memorial is never closed to the public; it is open 24 hours a day, 365 days a year. Each year, an estimated 6 million people visit the memorial. Admission is free.

Certainly, maintenance of the huge stone monument is expensive. In 2013, the National Park Service spent more than $2 million to maintain the memorial.

Several types of stone were used in the memorial's construction. Limestone from Indiana was used for the interior walls and columns. Marble from Alabama was used for the ceiling, while the pedestal and platform were made with marble from Tennessee. The *foundation* and floor slabs are composed of poured concrete. Marble for the exterior walls was obtained in Colorado, and some of the huge blocks used for those walls weigh as much as 23 tons each.

The building is 188 feet long and 118 feet wide. It rises 99 feet from its foundation. Each column is 44 feet high. The memorial sits on 107 acres at the western end of the National Mall, overlooking the Potomac River.

The statue of Lincoln was fashioned from marble found in Georgia. The statue weighs 175 tons.

Behind the statue are carved these words: "In this temple as in the hearts of the people for whom he saved the Union the memory of Abraham Lincoln is enshrined forever." Those words were written by Royal Cortissoz, the art critic for the *New York Tribune* newspaper. He was a long-time friend of Henry Bacon.

The names of the 36 states in the Union during Lincoln's presidency are etched over the columns, but the names of all states do appear in the memorial. In 1922, when the memorial was dedicated, the names of the 48 states in the Union at that time were etched in a decorative border along the roofline. Later, a plaque was added to the memorial that included the names of Alaska and Hawaii, both of which were admitted as states in 1959.

Following the assassination at Ford's Theater in Washington, President Lincoln was buried in his hometown in Springfield,

Make Connections

Construction of the Lincoln Memorial ran over budget. It cost $2,957,000, about a third more than planned.

Dr. Martin Luther King Jr. is visible from behind at the lower left corner of this photograph. On August 28, 1963, more than 250,000 people came to Washington, D.C., to ask Congress to pass civil rights laws. The crowd that gathered in front of the Lincoln Memorial to hear King was so large that it stretched from the steps of the memorial to the Washington Monument, about a half-mile away.

Free at Last

In 1955, a weary black seamstress named Rosa Parks refused to give up her seat on a crowded bus to a white man. In refusing to give up her seat, Parks had broken one of the Jim Crow laws in Montgomery, Alabama. Nearly a century after the Civil War, many states still observed the laws that denied blacks the same rights guaranteed to whites.

Rosa Parks was arrested and taken to jail. She was soon bailed out by friends.

Word of the arrest spread throughout the black community in Montgomery. Black leaders met at the Dexter Avenue Baptist Church in Montgomery and planned a boycott of the Montgomery bus system. The black leaders who met at Dexter Avenue Baptist that night also elected the minister of the church to lead what would become known as the Montgomery Bus Boycott. That minister was Dr. Martin Luther King Jr.

No black would ride a bus in Montgomery until the city's bus company ensured that blacks would be just as entitled to seats as whites. The Montgomery Bus Boycott is regarded as the beginning of the modern civil rights movement in America. Eventually, the U.S. Supreme Court ordered the bus system in Montgomery desegregated. In the meantime, blacks had stayed off the Montgomery buses for more than a year.

"A miracle had taken place," King wrote after the boycott ended. "The once dormant Negro community was now fully awake." Blacks now intended to take seriously the words that had been carved into walls of the Lincoln Memorial.

On the north wall of the memorial, Bacon had ordered the text of Lincoln's Second Inaugural Address etched into the marble. The address had been written and delivered in the final months of the Civil War. Lincoln intended the speech to mark the beginning of the long healing process he knew would be ahead of the Union once the cease-fire had been declared.

The Second Inaugural Address said, in part: "With *malice* toward none, with charity for all, with firmness in the right as God gives us to see the right, let us finish the work we are in, to bind up the nation's wounds, to care for him who shall have borne the battle, and for his widow and orphans, to do all which may achieve and cherish a just and a lasting peace among ourselves and with all nations."

Leaders of the Civil Rights movement in America found the words on the south wall of the memorial even more stirring. Those words were taken from the Gettysburg Address, delivered by Lincoln on November 19, 1863, on the day a national cemetery was dedicated on the Gettysburg battlefield in Pennsylvania. On the first three days of July 1863, Union forces defeated a huge Confederate army at Gettysburg, turning the war finally in the Union's favor. In his speech, Lincoln said, "Fourscore and seven years ago our fathers brought forth on this continent a new nation, conceived in liberty and dedicated to the proposition that all men are created equal."

This is the first page of one of Lincoln's drafts of the speech he would give at the dedication of the Gettysburg battlefield cemetery in November 1863. The brief speech—just 272 words—would become known as the Gettysburg Address.

By the early 1960s, African Americans had won many important battles in their journey toward equality. The United States government was slowly living up to the words Lincoln had spoken at Gettysburg. In 1954 the U.S. Supreme Court had ruled in *Brown v. Board of Education* that schools could no longer be segregated. The Supreme Court also struck down the Jim Crow laws by ordering the Montgomery buses desegregated.

Even the Daughters of the American Revolution came around. In 1964, the DAR invited Marian Anderson to sing at Constitution Hall. She agreed and gave one of the final concerts of her career on the stage where she had been banned a quarter-century before.

Later, Anderson said, "It was a beautiful concert hall and I was happy to sing in it."

Still, many government leaders in America resisted the idea that blacks deserved equal treatment. In 1958, President Dwight D. Eisenhower was forced to send federal troops to Little Rock, Arkansas, to accompany nine black students who wished to enroll in Little Rock High School. A year later, Arkansas Governor Orval Faubus closed the school briefly so he would not have to admit black students to what had been a whites-only school.

In 1962, United States marshals held back a mob of angry whites as black student James Meredith enrolled at the University of Mississippi. And in 1963, Alabama Governor George Wallace stood in the doorway at the University of Alabama to prevent black students James

George Wallace (standing at podium), the governor of Alabama, reads a statement at the entrance to the University of Alabama. President John F. Kennedy called in the National Guard to make sure African-American students were admitted to the university.

Hood and Vivian Malone from enrolling there. President John F. Kennedy ordered Alabama National Guard troops onto the University of Alabama campus to accompany the students as they registered for classes. Wallace reluctantly stepped aside.

That night, President Kennedy spoke to the nation on television. He said, "I am asking Congress to enact legislation giving all Americans the right to be served in facilities which are open to the public—hotels, restaurants, theaters, retail stores and similar establishments." Later, Congress would respond to the president's request by drafting the Civil Rights Act.

One man who saw the president on TV that night was A. Philip Randolph, who had founded the Brotherhood

Dr. Martin Luther King Jr. waves from the Lincoln Memorial during the March on Washington. King was one of the most influential leaders of the Civil Rights Movement in the 1950s and 1960s. He worked tirelessly to secure equal rights for all Americans. Martin Luther King was killed by an assassin on April 4, 1968, in Memphis, Tennessee.

of Sleeping Car Porters—a labor union representing black railroad workers. Randolph was moved by Kennedy's words, and organized what has come to be known as the "March on Washington"—a demonstration on the National Mall by black Americans calling for Congress to pass the Civil Rights laws Kennedy had outlined in his speech. "Let the nation and the world know the meaning of our numbers," Randolph said. "We are the advance guard of a massive moral revolution for jobs and freedom."

On August 28, 1963, more than 250,000 people crowded onto the National Mall. The highlight of the day was the speech given by Dr. Martin Luther King Jr. Since the Montgomery Bus Boycott King had become the nation's most important voice for Civil Rights.

Make Connections

Asa Philip Randolph was a black leader who worked for civil rights during the 1950s, '60s, and '70s. He came up with the idea of the March on Washington after watching President John F. Kennedy's speech on television in the spring of 1963.

King delivered his speech on the steps of the Lincoln Memorial, including these famous words:

> I have a dream that my four little children will one day live in a nation where they will not be judged by the color of their skin, but by the content of their character. . . . I have a dream when all God's children, black men and white men, Jews and gentiles, Protestants and Catholics, will be able to join hands and sing in the words of the old Negro spiritual: "Free at last. Free at last. Thank God almighty, we are free at last."

Text-Dependent Question
What did the Supreme Court decide in the case *Brown v. Board of Education of Topeka, Kansas*?

Research Project
The Montgomery Bus Boycott was a major event in the history of the Civil Rights Movement. Why did African Americans in Alabama believe a boycott was needed in 1955? Did the boycott work out the way that Civil Rights leaders intended?

Chronology

1860 Abraham Lincoln is elected the 16th president of the United States on November 6, defeating three candidates; in December, South Carolina announces it will leave the United States, and six other Southern states soon follow.

1861 Lincoln is sworn in as president on March 4; Confederate troops fire on Fort Sumter, South Carolina, on April 12.

1863 Lincoln issues the Emancipation Proclamation on January 1, which frees all the slaves in the rebellious states.

1865 On April 9 Robert E. Lee surrenders his Confederate army to Ulysses S. Grant at Appomattox Court House; on April 14 Lincoln is assassinated at Ford's Theater in Washington by John Wilkes Booth.

1867 In March, Congress establishes the Lincoln Monument Association; it fails to raise funds and is disbanded.

1911 U.S. Senator Shelby Cullom and House Speaker Joseph G. Cannon convince Congress to appropriate $2 million for the Lincoln Memorial.

1912 Potomac Park at the western end of the National Mall is chosen as the site of the Lincoln Memorial on February 13.

1913 Henry Bacon is hired to design the Lincoln Memorial.

1914 Work begins on the memorial on February 12.

1922 The Lincoln Memorial is dedicated on May 30.

1939 Singer Marian Anderson performs on the steps of the Lincoln Memorial on April 9.

1963 More than 250,000 people participate in the March on Washington and hear Martin Luther King Jr. deliver his "I Have a Dream" speech on August 26.

2009 On February 12, diplomats and citizens assemble in the Lincoln Memorial chamber to honor Abraham Lincoln on 200th anniversary of his birth.

2013 On July 26, the memorial is briefly closed after a vandal splashes the Lincoln statue's base and legs with green paint.

Series Glossary

capstone—a stone used at the top of a wall or other structure.

cornerstone—the first stone placed at a spot where two walls meet, usually considered the starting point of construction.

dome—an element of architecture that resembles the hollow upper half of a sphere.

edifice—a large building with an imposing appearance.

facade—the decorative front of a building.

foundation—the stone and mortar base built below ground that supports a building, bridge, monument, or other structure.

hallowed—holy, consecrated, sacred, or revered.

keystone—the architectural piece at the crown of a vault or arch which marks its apex, locking the other pieces into position.

memorial—something designed to help people remember a person or event in history.

obelisk—a shaft of stone that tapers at the peak.

pantheon—a public building containing monuments to a nation's heroes.

pedestal—the base or support on which a statue, obelisk, or column is mounted.

portico—a roof supported by columns, usually extending out from a building.

rotunda—a large and high circular hall or room in a building, usually surmounted by a dome.

standard—a flag or banner that is adopted as an emblem or symbol by a nation.

symbol—an item that represents or stands for something else.

Further Reading

Aretha, David. *Sit-ins and Freedom Rides*. Greensboro, N.C.: Morgan Reynolds Publishing, 2009.

Freedman, Russell. *Freedom Walkers: The Story of the Montgomery Bus Boycott*. New York: Holiday House Publishers, 2008.

Hardy, Sheila Jackson, and P. Stephen Hardy. *Extraordinary People of the Civil Rights Movement*. Danbury, Conn.: Children's Press, 2007.

Hasday, Judy L. *Women in the Civil Rights Movement*. Philadelphia: Mason Crest, 2012.

McPherson, James M. *Abraham Lincoln*. New York: Oxford University Press, 2009.

Nelson, Kristin L. *The Lincoln Memorial*. Minneapolis: Lerner, 2004.

Oates, Stephen B. *With Malice Toward None: A Life of Abraham Lincoln*. New York: HarperPerennial, 2011.

Perry, LaVora. *A History of the Civil Rights Movement*. Philadelphia: Mason Crest, 2013.

Phibbs, Cheryl Fisher. *The Montgomery Bus Boycott: A History and Reference Guide*. Santa Barbara, Calif.: ABC-CLIO, 2009.

Rodriguez, Junius P. *Slavery in the United States: A Social, Political, and Historical Encyclopedia*, Vol. 2. Santa Barbara, Calif.: ABC-CLIO, 2007.

Sacher, Jay. *Lincoln Memorial: The Story and Design of an American Monument*. Illus. by Chad Gowey. San Francisco: Chronicle Books, 2014.

White, Ronald C. Jr. *A. Lincoln: A Biography*. New York: Random House, 2009.

Internet Resources

http://www.nps.gov/linc

The National Park Service's website for the Lincoln Memorial includes photos, park information, facts about the memorial, and an interactive section.

http://www.civilwar.org/

Find out about the battlefields of the Civil War, take quizzes, and learn how you can help preserve the historic sites where Civil War battles occurred.

http://www.pbs.org/civilwar/

This companion website to the influential documentary by Ken Burns includes images of original Civil War photographs, historical documents, maps of key battles, research information, and more.

http://memory.loc.gov/ammem/cwphtml/cwphome.html

View images of more than 1,000 photographs of Civil War military personnel, preparations for battle, after-effects of battles, and portraits of Confederate and Union officers.

http://www.loc.gov/exhibits/brown/

Hosted by the Library of Congress, this website revisits the *Brown v. Board of Education* ruling. The site features photos of people and documents relating to the years before and after the 1954 order to desegregate public schools.

http://www.pbs.org/wgbh/amex/eyesontheprize

Based on the PBS American Experience television series *Eyes on the Prize: America's Civil Rights Movement 1954–1985*, this site links to profiles on people and documents from the time.

Index

American Revolution, 10
Anderson, Marian, 10, 11, 38
Arlington National Cemetery,
    18, 31

Bacon, Henry, 18, 22, 25, 26, 30,
    31, 36
Booth, John Wilkes, 13
Brown v. Board of Education, 38

Cannon, Joseph G., 15, 16
Civil Rights, 36-37, 40
Civil Rights Act, 39
Civil War, 9, 13, 17, 24, 25, 35,
    36
Constitution Hall, 10, 11, 38
Cortissoz, Royal, 30
Cullom, Shelby, 14, 15, 16, 22

Daughters of the American
    Revolution, 10, 11, 38
Dexter Avenue Baptist Church,
    35, 36

Eisenhower, Dwight D., 38

Faubus, Orval, 38
Ford's Theater, 13, 31
French, Daniel Chester, 21, 22-
    26

Gettysburg Address, 19, 27, 37
Guerin, Jules V., 26, 27

Harding, Warren G., 27

Hay, John, 17
Hood, James, 39
Hurok, Sol, 10
Ickes, Harold L., 11

Jefferson, Thomas, 17
Jim Crow laws, 9, 35, 38

Kennedy, John F., 39
King, Rev. Dr. Martin Luther Jr.,
    36, 40

L'Enfant, Pierre Charles, 17
Lincoln, Abraham
    and Civil War, 9, 13, 17, 24,
        25, 35, 36
    as "Great Emancipator," 14,
        18
    life of, 13-15, 19, 27, 30
Lincoln Memorial
    Layout of, 29-33
    Lincoln Memorial
        Commission, 16, 18, 24
    Lincoln Monument
        Association, 13, 14
    Maintenance of, 29
    Planning of, 13-27
Lincoln, Robert Todd, 31
Lincoln's Second Inaugural
    Address, 19, 36
Little Rock, Arkansas, 38

Malone, Vivian, 39
March on Washington, 40
McKim, Charles, 31

Index

Memorial Day, 27
Meredith, James, 38
Mills, Clarke, 13, 14
Montgomery Bus Boycott, 36, 40

National Mall, 11, 14, 17, 22, 27,
    30, 40
National Park Service, 29, 33
New York City, 10

Parks, Rosa, 35
Philadelphia, 10
Piccirillis brothers, 26
Potomac Park, 18
Potomac River, 17, 22, 30, 31

Randolph, A. Philip, 40

Reflecting Pool, 31, 32
Roosevelt, Eleanor, 11
Springfield, IL, 31

Taft, William Howard, 16

Union Baptist Church, 10
United States Congress, 13, 16

Wallace , George, 38
Washington, D.C., 10, 11, 13,
    25, 31
Washington, George, 17, 18
Washington Monument, 14, 16,
    31, 32
White House, 17, 24

Picture Credits

page
1:    used under license from
        Shutterstock, Inc.
3:    used under license from
        Shutterstock, Inc.
8:    Library of Congress
12:   Library of Congress
15:   Hulton/Archive
19:   used under license from
        Shutterstock, Inc.
20:   used under license from
        Shutterstock, Inc.

23:   Hulton/Archive
25:   Corbis
28:   used under license from
        Shutterstock, Inc.
31:   Joseph Sohm; ChromoSohm
        Inc./Corbis
32:   Library of Congress
34:   Hulton/Archive
37:   National Archives
39:   Library of Congress
40:   Hulton/Archive

Contributors

BARRY MORENO has been librarian and historian at the Ellis Island Immigration Museum and the Statue of Liberty National Monument since 1988. *The Statue of Liberty Encyclopedia* (2000), *The Encyclopedia of Ellis Island* (2004), *Ellis Island's Famous Immigrants* (2008), and *The Ellis Island Quiz Book* (2011). He also co-edited a scholarly study on world migration called *Leaving Home: Migration Yesterday and Today* (2011). His biography has been included in *Who's Who Among Hispanic Americans*, *The Directory of National Park Service Historians*, *Who's Who in America*, and *The Directory of American Scholars*. Mr. Moreno lives in New York City.

HAL MARCOVITZ has written more than 100 books for young readers. He lives in Chalfont, Pennsylvania, with his wife, Gail. They have two grown daughters, Ashley and Michelle.